SOLOS
for the
CELLO
PLAYER

With Piano Accompaniment

Selected and Edited by

OTTO DERI

Ed. 2313

G. SCHIRMER, Inc.

DISTRIBUTED BY

HAL•LEONARD®
CORPORATION
7777 W. BLUEMOUND RD. P.O. BOX 13819 MILWAUKEE, WI 53213

The 17 pieces contained in this volume present material on the intermediate level. The pieces have been selected so that various stylistic periods (baroque, classic, romantic, impressionistic) are represented. The selections appear in order of difficulty.

Many of the compositions are original cello works. The other selections are adaptations or transcriptions, which should broaden the somewhat limited cello repertory. The fingerings and bowings have been revised by the editor according to the principles of modern cello technique.

CONTENTS

Index by Composers

1. Lullaby

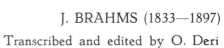

J. BRAHMS (1833—1897)
Transcribed and edited by O. Deri

44420 cx

2. Nina

(Canzonetta)

G. B. PERGOLESI (1710—1736)

Andantino

44420

3. Andante

(from "Orfeo")

C.W. von GLUCK (1714—1787)

4. La Cinquantaine

(Air in the olden Style)

G. MARIE (1852—1928)

44420

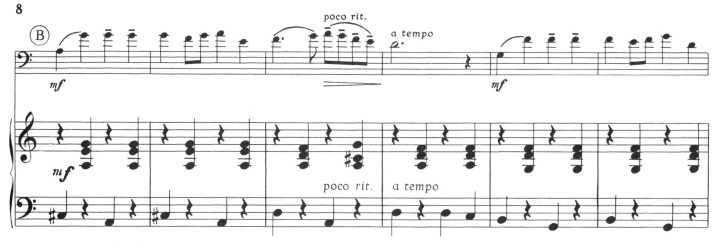

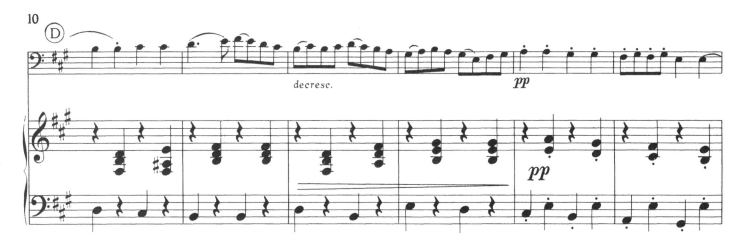

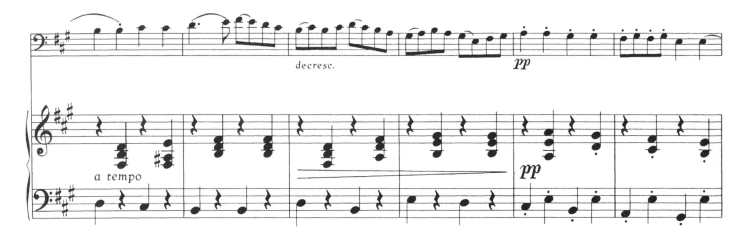

5. Romance

C. DEBUSSY (1862—1918)

6. Larghetto

(from Violin Sonata, Op. 1, No. 13)

G. F. HANDEL (1685—1759)

Transcribed and edited by O. Deri

Larghetto

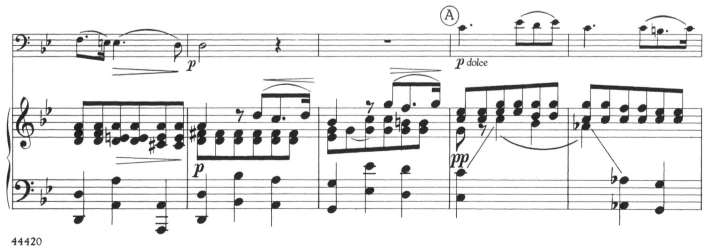

44420

7. Aria

A. LOTTI (1667—1740)

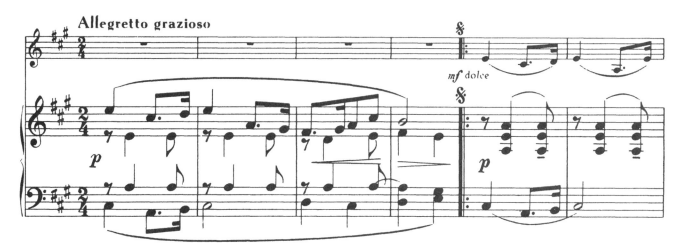

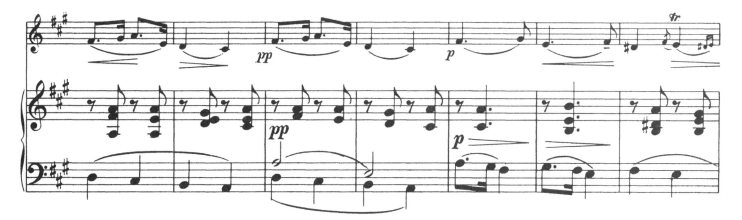

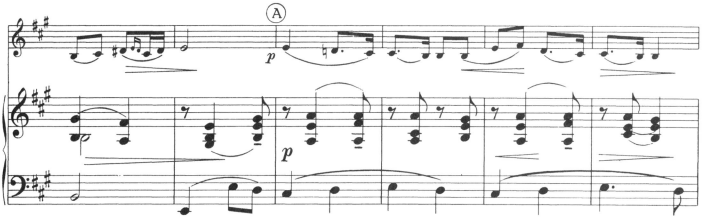

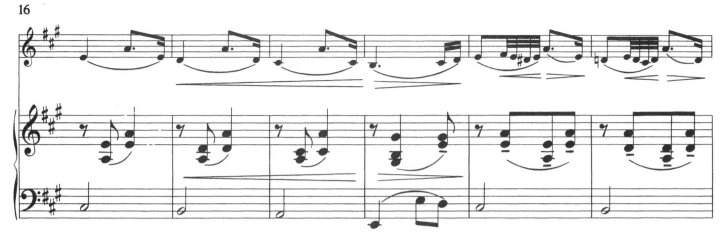

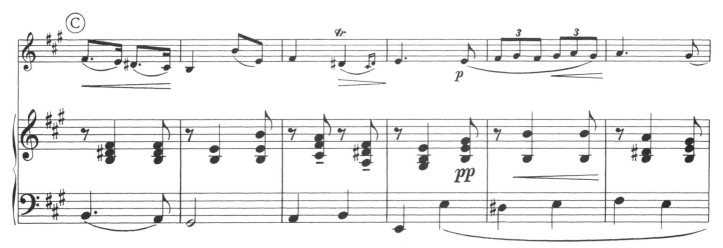

8. Lento

(from Five Pieces in Popular Mood)

R. SCHUMANN (1810—1856)

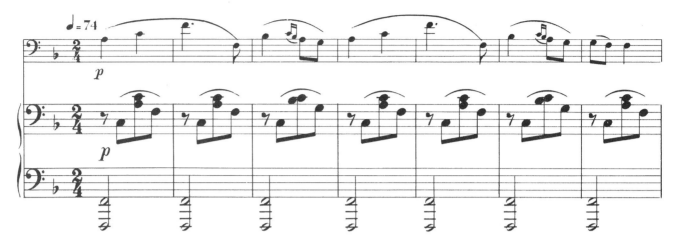

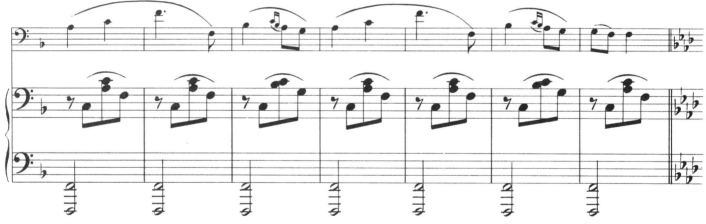

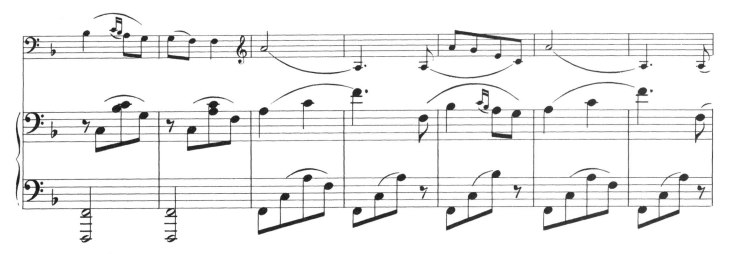

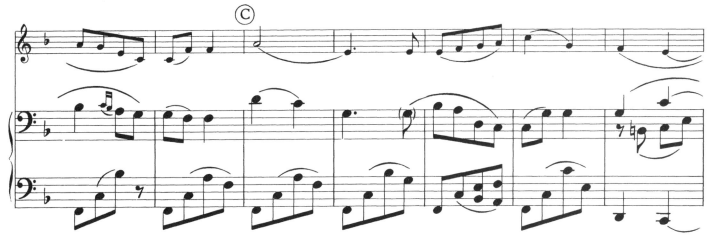

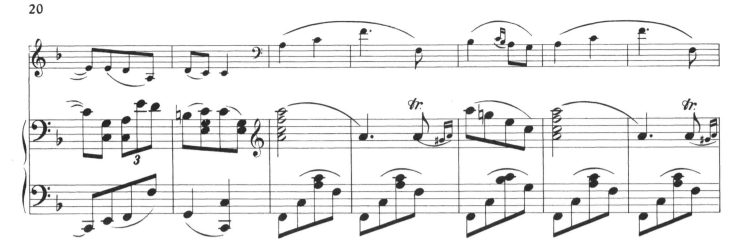

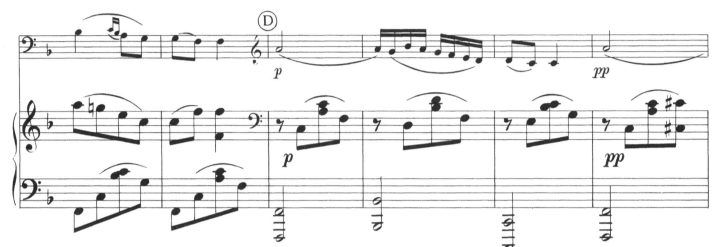

9. Bourrée I and II

BOURRÉE I   (from Third Cello Suite)

J. S. BACH (1685—1750)

Poco Allegro

BOURRÉE II

BOURRÉE I

44420

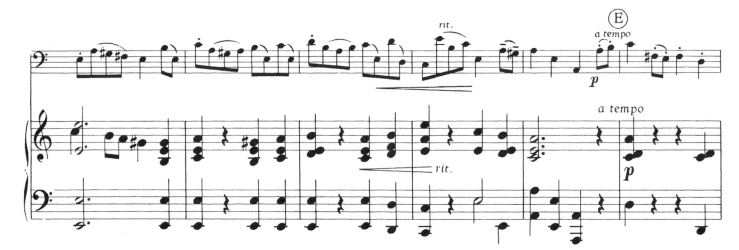

10. Andante

L. van BEETHOVEN (1770—1827)
Transcribed and edited by O. Deri

Andante grazioso con moto

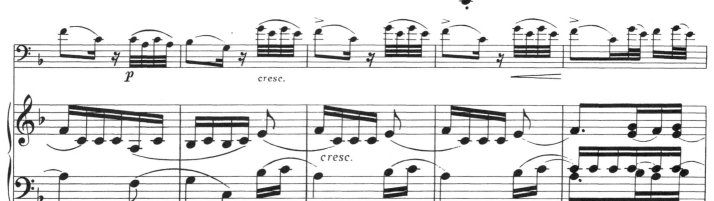

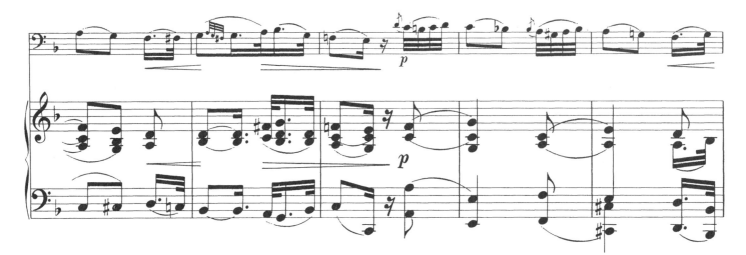

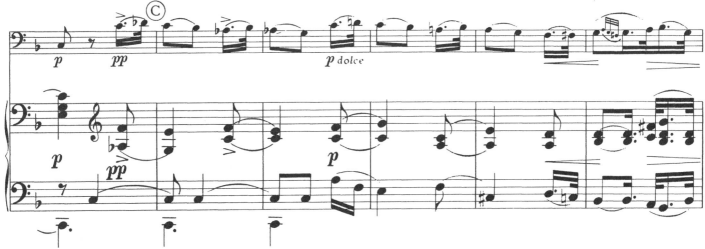

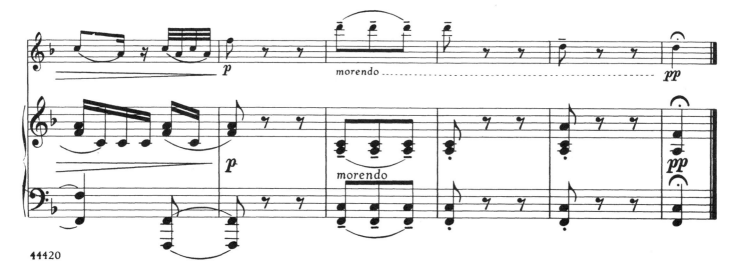

11. The Swan

(from "The Carnival of Animals")

C. SAINT-SAËNS (1835—1921)

44420

12. Menuet

(from Divertimento in D, K. 334)

W. A. MOZART (1756—1791)

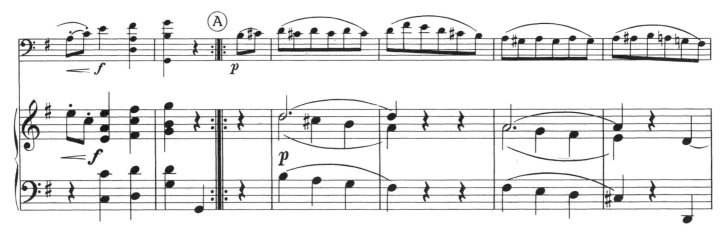

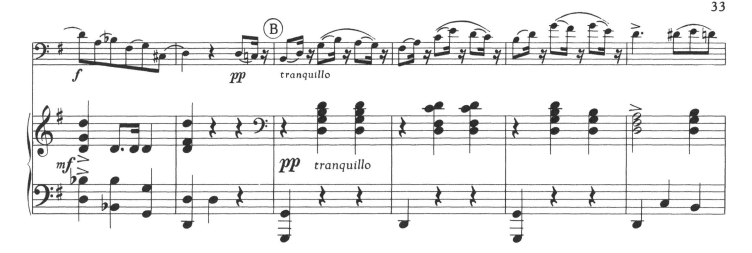

44420

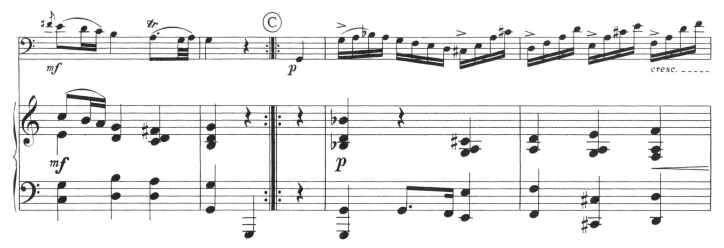

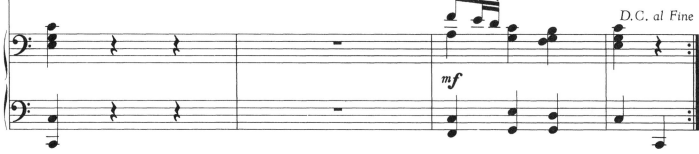

13. Sicilienne

G. FAURE, Op. 78 (1830--1914)

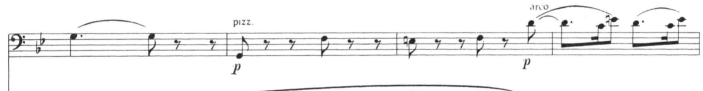

44420

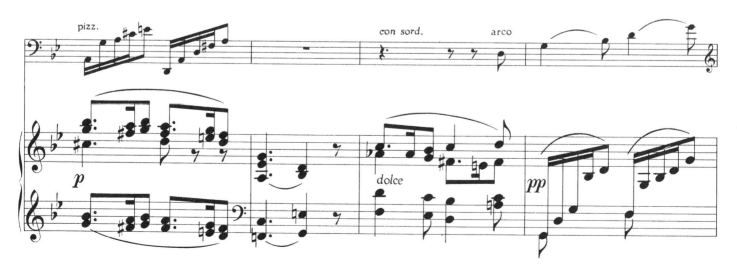

14. Allegro

(from Violin Sonata, Op. 1, No. 15)

G. F. HANDEL (1685—1759)
Transcribed and edited by O. Deri

44420

15. Village Song

D. POPPER, Op. 62, No. 2 (1846—1913)

Allegretto

44420

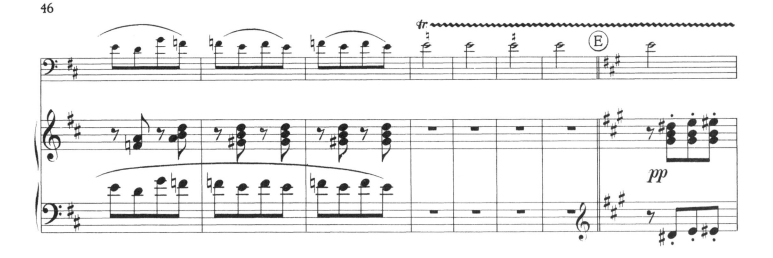

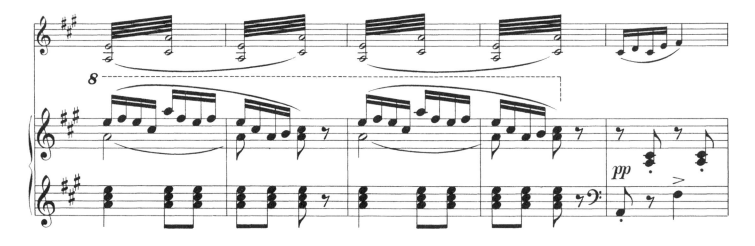

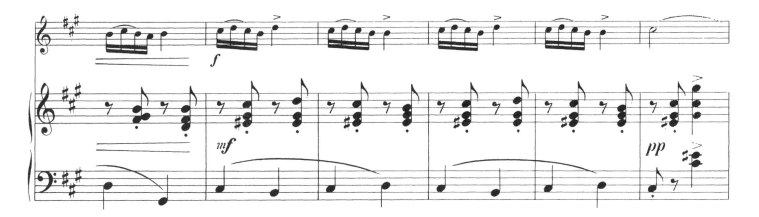

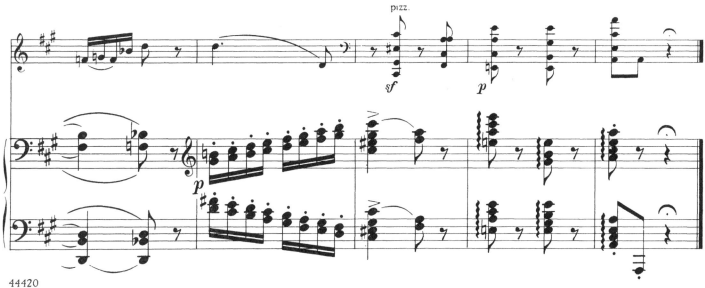

44420

16. Allegro Spiritoso

Jean Baptiste Senaillé (1687—1730)

44420

44420

17. Country Dance

C. M. von WEBER (1786—1826)
Transcribed and edited by O. Deri

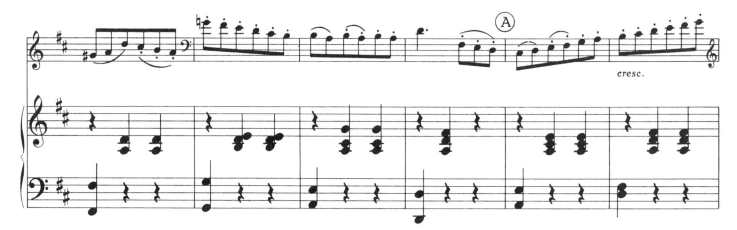

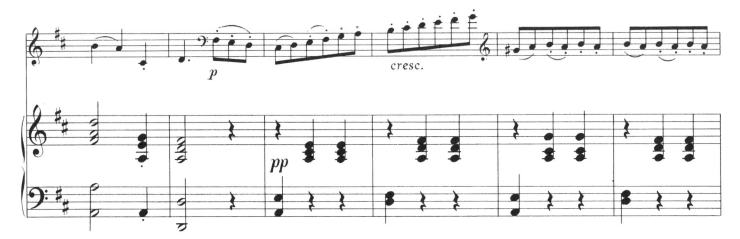

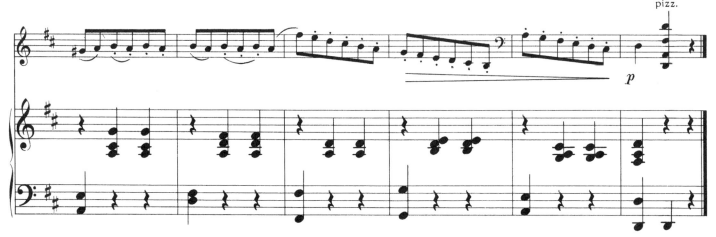

44420